David Benoit

Etudes for the Contemporary Pianist

for Piano

HENDON MUSIC

BOOSEY & HAWKES

AN IMAGEM COMPANY

DISTRIBUTED BY
HAL•LEONARD®
CORPORATION
7777 W. BLUEMOUND RD. P.O. BOX 13819 MILWAUKEE, WI 53213

www.boosey.com
www.halleonard.com

Published by Hendon Music, Inc.
a Boosey & Hawkes company
229 West 28th Street, 11th Fl
New York NY
10001

www.boosey.com

First printed 2009

ETUDES

for the contemporary pianist

A collection of short pieces for pianists of all ages
composed by **David Benoit**

CONTENTS

COMPOSER'S NOTES

1. Journey in a Rental Car

The opening F repetition signifies the warning chime before the seat belt is fastened.

In this instance, the journey in a rental car (some generic American brand) originates at Los Angeles International Airport and ends at Villa Montalvo, the former mayor of San Francisco's summer Mediterranean estate. This was the first Etude composed during my stay there as an "artist-in-residence."

2. I Miss You

This is a poetic little piece that begins very simply with a sense of longing and sadness. The brief right hand eruption in the middle signifies the loneliness and frustration of the composer's unmet desires.

3. A Solitary Moment by the Ocean

My first classical piano piece as a kid growing up was Schumann's "Chopin" from *Carnival*. I loved this piece with its beautiful rolling left hand. This is my homage not necessarily to Schumann but to Chopin written in the style of some of his nocturnes.

4. Lonely Boy

The title is self-explanatory.

5. Scherzo for Charles Brown

Charles Schulz actually had two friends named Charles Brown growing up. I don't know which one provided the inspiration for "Peanuts" but does it matter? There is a little bit of Vince Guaraldi in there as the piece reveals itself but the beginning may be more reminiscent of "Peanuts Gallery" Concerto by composer Ellen Taaffe Zwilich.

6. Kenji

"Kenji" is a piece about a young Japanese boy that was adopted by my good friend Kent Nagano's cousin, Karen Nagano and Rick Deragon. Karen is a brilliant oil on canvas artist in the Napa Valley who we commissioned to do a rendering of our daughter June. Kenji and June were adopted from the same host family in Hiroshima, Japan.

7. Betty's Dance

This piece started with a different title, but the more I played it, the more it reminded me of my mother Betty who died in 1997. My mother loved Stephen Sondheim whose music provided the inspiration for this composition. I miss her terribly.

8. Fallen Peacock

First of all, I hate peacocks. We are under siege with them in our Palos Verdes neighborhood. They are messy and loud and keep us up all night. Having said that, one managed to fly into our yard and crash into a wall. It tried and tried to get up and fly away but couldn't…

JOURNEY IN A RENTAL CAR

DAVID BENOIT

2

I MISS YOU

DAVID BENOIT

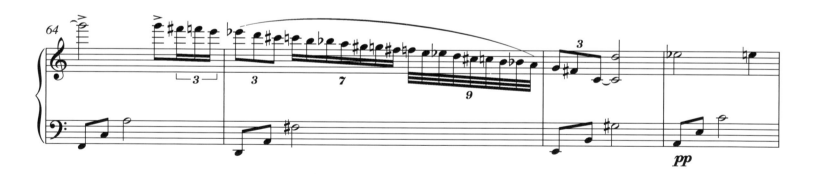

D.S. AL FINE

A SOLITARY MOMENT BY THE OCEAN

Composed by David Benoit

Adagio ♩.= ca.44

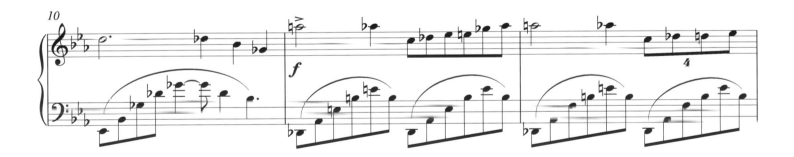

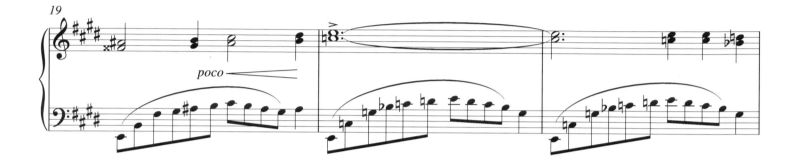

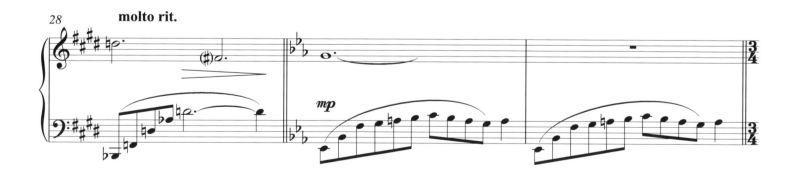

Più mosso
on D.S., slightly faster

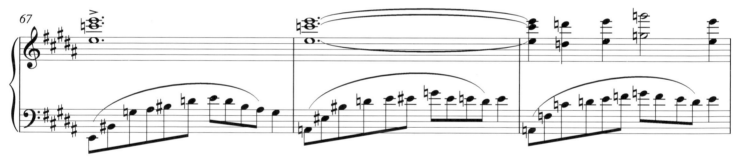

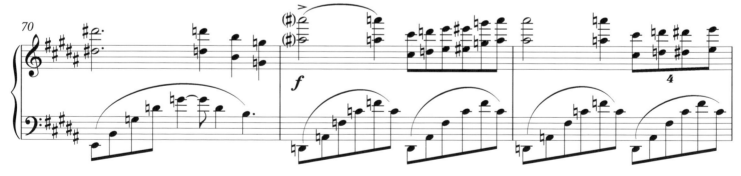

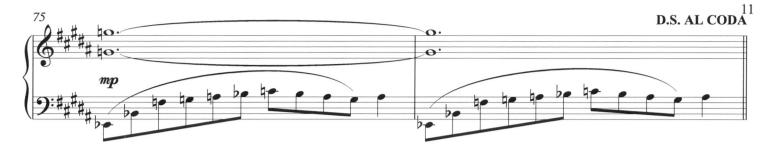

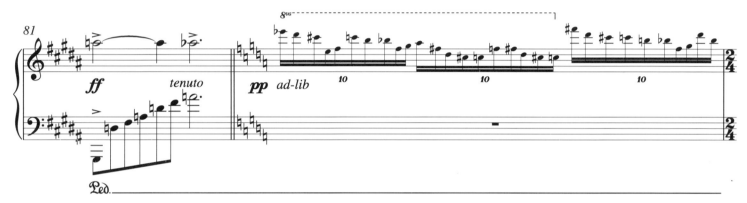

molto rall.

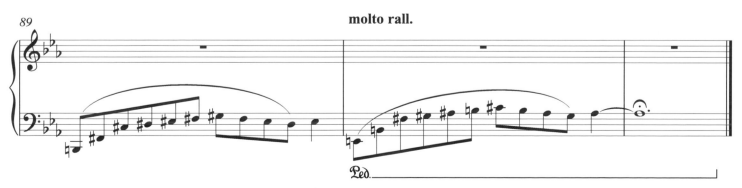

LONELY BOY

DAVID BENOIT

SCHERZO
for Charles Brown

DAVID BENOIT

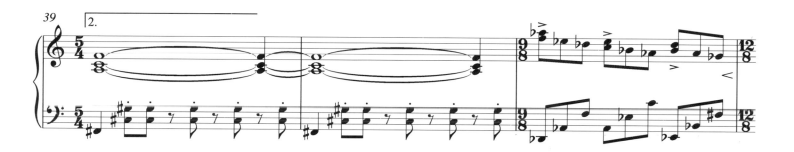

D.C. AL CODA

Optional ending

KENJI

DAVID BENOIT

Playful with a slightly blues feel ♩ = 80

Piano

Waltz tempo - allegro assai

Tempo primo

D.C. al FINE

BETTY'S DANCE

DAVID BENOIT

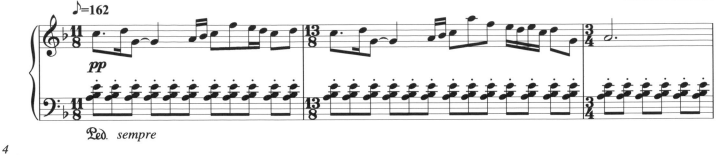

20

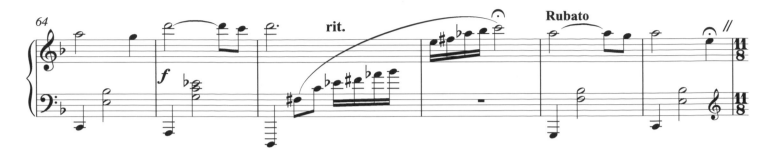

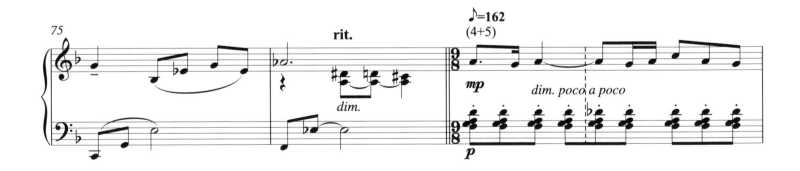

PEACOCK FALLEN

DAVID BENOIT

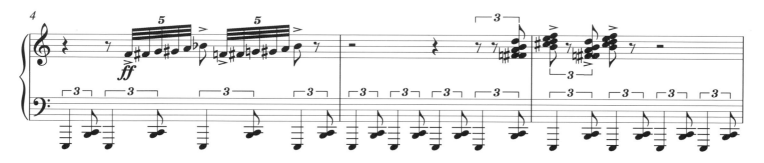

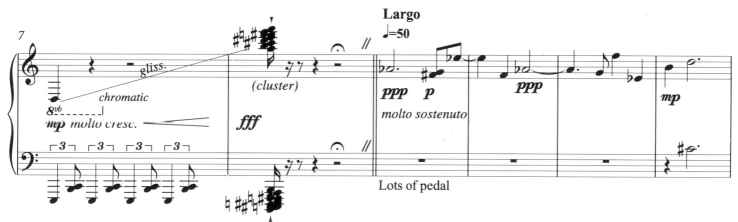

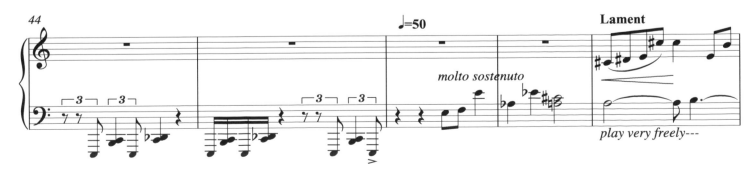